Undeserving Grace

"Met Husband While Foster Parenting"

Chanel Brantley

DEDICATION

This book is dedicated to my amazing sister Anna Hampton who cherishes reading as her favorite pastim~~e.e. It was~~ Anna ~~who~~ encouraged me during the long, challenging ~~difficult~~ years of singleness to persevere and have hope in the Lord.

CONTENTS

Contents

No table of contents entries found.

Forward

I have written this book to offer hope for single Christian men and women who desire to marry but are currently in a time of waiting. People have encouraged me to write a book about meeting my husband. I~~Well,~~ let's j~~j~~ust say it's not a fairy tale; but my story is true and may inspire others to trust God's timing. His ways are certainly better than ours. My story will reveal God's grace and goodness.

My Background

First, let's go back a few decades. I was born on June 26th, 1978 to Kerby and Katherine Rich. My parents were both believers at the time of my birth. From a very young age, my father taught me the truths of God's Word. The young, the middle-aged, and the elderly all need to read and study God's Word; we should have the attitude that we can ALL learn something new. Mother was a loving, compassionate parent who showed unfailing love to her children. Though Dad was a God-fearing man who spent many years of his life as a minister, Dad was a strict disciplinarian. Hence, as I grew up, I, unfortunately, couldn't reason ~~rationally~~ that my heavenly Father was very gracious and forgiving.

God blessed my parents with six children. All of my siblings have unique personalities with various talents and gifts. Family gatherings at Thanksgiving and Christmas definitely wouldn't be considered dull. To describe my siblings, I will start with Anna, the first-born child. I remember Anna as a~~the~~ gracious, self-sacrificing sister who put other people's needs above her own. Robert was a~~the~~ brilliant, analytical brother. Penny was a~~the~~ creative sister with the best sense of humor; yes, we sure need ~~the~~ humor to get us through life. Lisa was a cheerful, friendly sister. Doreen was a beautiful, kind sister.

M~~When I was a child,~~ my father was a military chaplain when I was a child, ~~;~~ so we moved around often. As a result, having life-long friends was not easy.~~Having life-long friends was not easy.~~ I graduated from Tri-City Christian School in Vista, California, in 1997 and then attended Pensacola Christian   College   in   the   fall   of   1997.

Life after High School

College days were filled with tests, projects, community service, and part-time work. College is not meant for everyone, but it certainly helps prepare young people for life. I thought ~~that~~ I would meet my husband at college, and though there were plenty of handsome young men at Pensacola Christian College, most of them were dating other people. I had many casual dates during my college years, but they were not the right fit for me. I graduated from Pensacola Christian College in May of 2003 and shortly afterward began teaching kindergarten at a Christian school in Georgia.

Children are miracles from God and should be valued as such. Their minds absorb so much information! Children will become the doctors, lawyers, nurses, police officers, dentists, and veterinarians of tomorrow. We should certainly be careful of how we treat children, for ~~, for~~ years later, they will remember the individuals who were rude, impatient, or harsh with words. Perhaps you're familiar with the verse which says, "*But Jesus said, 'Let the little children come to Me, and do not forbid them: for of such is the kingdom of heaven.'" Matthew 19:14.* It is important that those who consider teaching as a career have a love for their students.

Working ~~Forfor~~ <u>for</u> Mesa Airlines

Unfortunately, my first year of teaching did not go very well, so I decided to take a job as a flight attendant for Mesa Airlines. Mesa Airlines was a co-share partner with United Airlines, U.S. Airways, and American West Airlines. Although I was employed by Mesa Airlines, I wore the U.S. Airways uniform.

After the terrorist attack on September 11th, 2001, Mesa Airlines required extensive training for flight attendants. Most of my training took place in Phoenix, Arizona, where I met my roommate Melissa, who was also training to be a flight attendant. She was a typical all-American girl ~~who was~~ determined to become a successful flight attendant. She had the self-confidence that could help her reach many goals in life, yet I remember that she would become easily offended. Growing up with many siblings, I got spanked for arguing with my sisters, so I knew how to get along with people. But I soon learned that I should not be quick to judge others, something we can easily do.

After weeks of dealing with Melissa's quick offenses, I learned that Melissa's mother had been brutally murdered by a man who doused her with gasoline and then set her on fire … just because she had forgotten to give him his paycheck. Sadly, her mother lived for <u>several</u> ~~a number of~~ days before she died in agony in a hospital.

Authorities were able to arrest the man who set Melissa's mother on fire. Unfortunately, we often don't know what people are going through, nor do we always know what their past has been like. Even though I didn't have a lot of self-confidence as a flight attendant, I remember Melissa emphasizing the importance of being self-confident when dealing with the public.

Working as a flight attendant was an interesting job. Flying to different cities in the United States and meeting new people was enjoyable. However, I didn't like the random work hours. I had to bid for my hours and didn't have a consistent work schedule. By bid, that means a person would submit specific work hours to the flight attendant website, and if the person was lucky, he or she would be granted the work hours ~~that were~~ submitted. I was raised by parents who did not drink alcohol. Drinking alcohol off-duty was readily accepted in the flight attendant world, and that was not something I wanted to inherit as part of my lifestyle. Scripture does not forbid ~~the drinking of~~drinking wine, but I wasn't accustomed to the worldly lifestyles that most flight attendants lived. I also began to see more homosexuals in the flight industry, and homosexuality was not a lifestyle among the people I grew up with. My mother told me, "You'll get tired of being a flight attendant, and you'll want to go back to teaching." I didn't believe my mother's words at the time, but she was right.

My Teaching Years

At twenty-seven years of age, I began teaching again, this time in a Christian school in North Carolina. Of all the states that I have lived in, North Carolina was my favorite. Western North Carolina has beautiful mountains, rivers, valleys, and plenty of friendly people. It also has great places for camping, hiking, ~~and~~ swimming and; there are many gorgeous waterfalls. ~~as well.~~ It was easy to make friends there, and my students' parents sometimes invited me into their homes for supper. I met my pastor's son, and we dated for several months; his kind personality, handsome looks, and Christ-like character attracted me to him. However, after months of dating, I realized some of his convictions were not the same as mine. I saw too many red flags, and a wise friend told me, "Make sure you love him." Although it was difficult to break off the relationship, it was a mutual breakup. Looking back, I know that I made the right decision.

It's normal to wish for that "special someone" to be by your side, for even Scripture says, *"It is not good that man should be alone" Genesis 2:18.* Fearing that I would not be able to find a Christian husband in a small town, I decided to go back to college to work on my master's degree, but my main goal was to work on my "Mrs." degree! After two years at Bob Jones University, I earned a master's degree in elementary education. It was frustrating spending two years writing papers, studying for tests and going on occasional dates but having no fiancé or engagement ring.

In the summer of 2011, I signed a teaching contract with a Christian school in Bristol, Tennessee. As a single, moving to a city where some people are not very friendly wasn't easy; others have indicated that they've also encountered unfriendly people there. ~~encountered unfriendly people there as well.~~ On a brighter note, there are many amazing Christian people in Bristol and the surrounding area, but it took a while to make friends with people who had the same beliefs and convictions as I did. *Proverbs 18:24* says, *"A man who has friends must himself be friendly."* Although some personalities won't click, sometimes we have to put forth an effort to make friends. By the time I moved to Bristol, most of the people I knew were already settled with their own friends, family, and careers. God did not create us to live solitary lives; people need each other in more ways than one. For singles, if the opportunity arises to go on a mission trip, take the opportunity and let God use you for His glory. Singleness is a gift from God; there are many benefits to being single, though people can be judgmental towards single or divorced people. Married people should reach out to those who live alone. Ladies can invite single ladies over to have dinner with their ~~family~~families.~~-~~ Or married men can invite single men over to have a meal as well. It's so easy to become self-absorbed with our lives, schedules, jobs, or vacation plans that we forget to include others.

There are many ways for followers of Christ to serve the Lord: take time for the widow, ~~the~~ widower, and those unable ~~who are not physically able~~ to leave their homes. Believers could teach Sunday school, prepare a meal for a church member, help with repairing items, mow a lawn, help clean the church, drive the church van, or work in the church nursery. These are just examples, yet there many other ~~other~~ ways in which the body of Christ works together to accomplish His purpose. Generally speaking, in today's society, married people are respected more than single people. However, I believe this should not be the case. Shouldn't those who exemplify Christ the most with their lives be respected more?

I remember my mother telling me ~~when I was~~ iinn my early thirties that I would marry at forty. I responded by saying, "That makes me very angry." Being angry about my state of singleness certainly didn't benefit me or anyone else; it reminds me of how God responded to Jonah. Those who are familiar with well-known Bible stories may recall how Jonah was angry that God did not destroy the people of Nineveh. God asked Jonah, *"Is it right for you to be angry?" Jonah 4:4.* Jonah's anger didn't benefit him one bit; unresolved anger leads to bitterness. After my mother told me that I would marry at forty, several~~a number of~~ years passed before God ~~would~~ fulfilled my deep desire to be a wife. Near Bristol, TN, I found Celebration Church with Pastor Robert Russell, who taught the truths of Scripture with a humble attitude. Celebration Church offered wonderful praise music, Wednesday evening meals~~ and~~, Bible classes, and a fellowship group for singles. Although there were good single men at church, most of the single men I had met in my thirties were either divorced or addicted to alcohol, drugs, or pornography. I did not want to drag harmful addictions into my marriage.

In hopes of finding a Christian husband at a social gathering, I sometimes attended ~~what was called~~ Contra-dancing, a form of folk dancing~~,~~ similar to ~~a~~ waltz or country line dancing. It is my personal conviction that there is nothing wrong with dancing as long as_it ~~the~~

~~dancing~~ is not done_ ~~-in-~~ sensually. ~~a sensual manner.~~ Though I met some single men at Contra-dancing gatherings, none of them had all the qualities I was hoping for.

Fortunately, a lot of my time as a single was spent in the classroom in a Christian school. Teaching young ~~children~~children, a curriculum that is based on Scripture is certainly beneficial. Although I enjoyed teaching second grade in Bristol, I remember difficult times for the children, parents, and teachers. To name a few, in my six years of service at Tennessee Avenue Christian Academy, one of my students lost a grandfather who had raised her, another student's father died after suffering a brain hemorrhage, another student- witnessed a murder, and a teenage student died after having heart complications. This was a lot of tragedy for my school to experience in six years!

Friends ~~From~~from The Father Above

Genuine life-long friends are hard to find and should not be taken for granted. After moving to Bristol, I prayed that God would give me good Christian friends. The first few years in a new city were lonely and difficult, and it was three years before God brought Glenda into my life. Glenda was different than the other women I knew. She had bright blue eyes, a cheerful smile, and a genuine joy within her soul. She was a good listener, self-sacrificing, optimistic, and considerate. Glenda wasn't a complainer, either, and it was evident that God's love shined through her. It's no wonder that she was her father's favorite child. I met Glenda on the Emmaus walk in Colonial Heights, Tennessee.

Often held at churches, Emmaus walks are similar to conferences or weekend retreats of spiritual renewal for those who have already accepted Christ as their Savior. During the Emmaus walk, we had a packed schedule of listening to many different women, singing praise songs to our God, praying for our needs, and of course, filling our bellies with delicious food. *Hebrews 10: 25* says, *"Not forsaking the assembling of ourselves together, as is the manner of some, but exhorting one another: and so much the more as you see the day approaching."*

When I was thirty-eight, I went on a few dates with a nice-looking Christian fellow. I was excited that someone of the opposite gender was actually interested in me. But I should have let him do the pursuing, for it wasn't long before he wasn't interested in a relationship. I recall him saying, "I'm not attracted to you anymore." Those were some unpleasant~~harsh tough~~ words to hear, and I was completely devastated. There were many nights I shed several tears and sometimes had trouble sleeping because I worried that I would never marry. But the truth of the matter is that it is far worse to be rejected by Christ than to be rejected by fallen men.

In the fall of 2017, I received a text message from Glenda. The text message indicated that God would provide a husband for me. I still had some doubts but knew that even though I was picky about finding a husband, I remembered God had been faithful to many women before me and provided the right men for them.

Foster Parenting

When I was thirty-nine, I sat in a women's conference one particular weekend at a church in Kingsport, Tennessee and heard of the great need for foster parents. The speaker used Scripture to promote the idea of helping those in need. I can't remember the exact verse, but perhaps it was *Deuteronomy 15: 11* which says, *"For the poor will never cease from the land; therefore, I command you, saying, 'You shall open your hand wide to your brother, to your poor and your needy, in your land."* Children placed in state custody certainly are needy. So, believing that God had opened the door for me to foster children, I embarked on the long process of legally becoming a foster parent. The Department of Children's Services required a background check, parenting classes, home visits, and the signing of several legal documents. With a home visit, a state worker would come to my house to make sure it was safe for children to live in: smoke detectors, fire extinguishers, and proper furniture for children had to be installed. Now, I don't agree with all of the policies of DCS, but I remember in one of the parenting classes, a woman gave excellent advice: "Do not be judgmental. Every one of you makes mistakes. Don't act like you haven't." We all certainly make mistakes … like the ones we wish no one knew about.

Everyone needs love and acceptance. Before I obtained legal custody of two young children, I prayed for children compatible with my personality. Have you heard the phrase "Be careful what you ask for"? On June 6th, 2018, I was granted legal custody of two very young and precious boys, a six-month-old infant and a twenty-month-old toddler. (Due to HIPPA privacy laws, I will refrain from using the children's legal names.) By this time, I worked an administrative assistant at a medical supply business in Blountville, TN. The infant had dark eyes, very curly blonde hair, and a laid-back personality. I was lucky to have an infant that rarely cried and usually slept through the night. The toddler with brown eyes and wavy blonde hair was an affectionate boy who liked being around people. My sister Anna came to visit us shortly after the boys were placed in my home; she cried the first time she saw them because the state had taken them away from their mother.

Thousands of children are in state custody in Tennessee, though the Department of Children's Services aims to reunite the children with a biological parent. In extreme cases of child abuse, parental rights are terminated, and DCS will place the child in the legal custody of a responsible person, sometimes a relative, who can care for the child.

The judge granted the boys' birth mother visitation rights on Saturdays. So, on some Saturdays, I would take the boys to meet their mother at the park or McDonald's. It was difficult for her to see her children but not be allowed to legally care for them.

The mother was kind, easygoing, and very cooperative; we never once argued or exchanged ugly words with each other. She told me, "I'm going to do everything I can to get my boys back," and put forth a lot of effort ~~to do so,~~ but that would take eight months. She cleaned her home, worked at Arby's, and took some parenting classes. It was my goal to work together as a team with the mother to ensure the physical and emotional well-being of the boys. My mother advised me not to take on two boys because she didn't think I could handle them all by myself. I thought to myself, "What could be worse than teaching twenty-second graders???" But I had forgotten that toddlers and babies make a lot of messes! There was a Christian daycare connected with the school where I had once taught; the daycare director knew me personally and agreed to keep the boys while I worked.

There were so many responsibilities as a single foster parent: wake the children up, feed the baby, get both boys ready in the morning, drop the boys off at daycare, pick the boys up, feed them supper, ~~give them a~~ bathe them, and the list goes on. Then there were routine doctor appointments, grocery shopping, meetings with my case worker, meetings with the boys' case worker, and appointments with the health clinic for WIC. On Friday evenings, I worked as a lifeguard at the YMCA for just a few months. Glenda, the friend I made on the Emmaus walk, would come and watch the boys. It became too much to keep up with three jobs ...taking care of the boys, my office job, and lifeguarding. Mother and I prayed that God would provide clothes for the boys to wear and praise God that it wasn't long before some women provided clothes for them! This reminds me of the verse which says, *"And my God shall supply all your needs according to His riches in glory in Christ Jesus" Philippians 4:19.*

It felt a little strange for the toddler to call me "mommy." But he desperately needed ~~was in desperate need of~~ a mother, and I was willing to temporarily fulfill that role for him. My parents ~~were~~ supported ~~ive of~~ my fostering, and they babysat the boys several times when I needed a helping hand. Dad certainly had patience with the toddler and would take time to play with him, and the toddler quickly grew to love and trust him. Many friends from church also~~There were also many friends from church who~~ helped babysit the boys if I needed an evening out. These people truly had a servant's heart and were willing to feed and bathe the boys and even change diapers. During the summer months, I took the boys to the park or let the toddler play in Glenda's pool; of course, we put floaters on him and kept a close eye on him.

Although being a foster parent forced me to not constantly dwell on my state of singleness, I remember crying on the phone to my mother one evening in August of 2018. I was so tired of being single and literally felt hopeless about finding a spouse. I told my mother that if God did not want me to be married, He needed to take away that desire. That ~~same~~ summer, I talked with my friend Alice at a playground while ~~the~~ thea toddler played close by. Alice was a cheerful woman with a strong faith in God, so it was easy to be drawn to her. As we sat at the playground, she told me, "God has someone for you." I looked at her with disbelief and didn't think that God would provide a husband for me as~~while being~~ a foster parent.

After Years ~~Of~~of Waiting

In October 2018, unfortunately, I lost ~~I, unfortunately, lost~~ my job at the medical supply business after missing some~~a number of~~ days of work. I thought to myself, "I'll never get married." But God was slowly unrolling the special plan He had for my life. He provided another job opening at the Christian daycare even before my office job ended. And the same week I lost my job, I started corresponding with my future husband through a dating website! I chose the dating website Farmers Only because I knew farmers were typically more conservative, and I had trouble finding a spouse on two other dating sites. But having legal custody of two boys would be a deterrent for some single men.

In the first email I received from Galen Brantley, who would later become my husband, I could tell that he wanted to find out my beliefs about divorce and remarriage. So, when I emailed him back, I mentioned the verse that indicates those who divorce and remarry commit adultery. However, to speak on behalf of those who have divorced and remarried, I certainly don't consider myself better than the divorced. I know several respectable people who ~~have divorced and later remarried, and~~divorced and later remarried, yet they've earned their place in society. All sinners need a Savior. I do believe that there is one exception for divorce, and that is adultery. I was skeptical about finding a decent Christian man on the internet, but ~~at forty years of age~~, I felt like I was running out of options, at forty years of age. ~~-~~And honestly, I was intrigued by Galen's profile.

Galen had accepted Christ as his Savior when he was thirty, his political views were conservative, and he had a great sense of humor. He was six feet tall, had blond hair, blue eyes, a slim build, and a handsome face. In the beginning, I thought Galen was some sort of dream that would never become a reality. Also, I was self-conscious about my figure, for it certainly wasn't shaped exactly like the movie stars, celebrities, and beautiful models displayed in fashion magazines. Within about a week of talking on the phone, I told Galen about the foster children, not knowing his response~~what his response would~~ be. To my surprise, the foster boys did not stop Galen from pursuing me. We discussed many important topics over the phone: our faith-based beliefs; the roles of a husband and wife; our views on politics; our future goals, habits, finances, eating habits; and other issues.

After talking for just a few weeks over the phone, we decided to meet in person. Even though we were in our forties, I knew it would be best for my parents to know about our meeting in person. Galen called my father and told him ~~that~~ he wanted to get to know his daughter; Dad had a background check completed on Galen before we met. Galen would be flying from Oklahoma to Tri-Cities Airport in Blountville, Tennessee, which was about 25 minutes from my house. We agreed ahead of time that he would stay at the Days Inn in Bristol. My sister Anna had agreed to watch the boys for a few days while Galen was in town. On Saturday, November 10th, 2018, I remember getting a phone call from Galen informing me that he had missed his flight. I immediately began to think that the relationship was not meant to be. His plane from Oklahoma City to Dallas, Fort Worth, arrived on time, but the airport wouldn't let passengers exit the plane right away, and he missed his connecting flight from Dallas to Knoxville, TN. Fortunately, he called later that day and explained that he had gotten another flight. I had my best blue jeans, and a red sweater picked out for our first date. But things don't always go as planned, especially when young children are in the picture! The baby had gotten my outfit dirty, and I had to wear something not quite as nice.

First-time impressions aren't always the best, and honestly, the first time Galen and I met, I wasn't all that impressed. Ladies, keep that in mind if you haven't met your man in shining armor yet! Try not to focus too much on outward appearance, for we know that looks always fade with time. Galen pulled up in a white rental pick-up truck and was wearing glasses; ~~it was~~ the glasses ~~that~~ were a deterrent for me. He smiled, and I could sense he was a kind man who would not harm me. Although I had taken a great risk in meeting a ~~complete~~ stranger off the internet, I knew there were still good men out there; a single good man can be hard to find.

Though I knew of many girls who met their husbands on a dating website, I would recommend trying to find a spouse at church, at college, or through mutual friends before resorting to the internet. However, I believe God IS still sovereign over the internet. If He wanted to wipe out the internet completely, He most certainly could! During the few days that Galen visited me, we attended church together, ate at local restaurants, visited a nearby park, watched a political film together, and I introduced him to Anna and her husband, Jim. Galen and I both had a sinus infection during his visit and kept coughing; that was another reason why I thought the relationship would not work!

On Tuesday, while the boys and I were at the daycare, Galen repaired a number of items in my townhouse: the kitchen sink, the shower head in the bathroom, the dryer, and the overhead light in the laundry room. After he had fixed so many things, I thought having him around wasn't such a bad idea! Many of our beliefs were the same, but ~~it was his natural gift of being a handyman that~~his natural gift of being a handyman won me over. Before he flew back to Oklahoma, he asked, "How long do you think a couple should date before getting married?" I said at least six months, but later during marriage counseling, I discovered that my pastor and his wife had dated only five months before they married! However, as a general rule of thumb, I would recommend that couples date at least one year before saying, "I do."

Galen and I made arrangements for me to fly to Oklahoma for Christmas. My kind boss told me not to tell anyone ~~that~~ I would_-~~be~~ misssing a few days of work, and my parents agreed to watch the boys while I visited Galen. Snow started to fall in_the evening. Dad drove me to the airport. I was lucky to catch my flight on Friday, December 21st, and my plane arrived around midnight when Galen met me at the airport. We decided to rent two separate hotel rooms for the night before heading to Galen's house, which was four hours from the airport. Galen already had his own house, and being a gentleman and a man of integrity, he chose to spend the night at his ~~parents'~~parent's house while I visited him. The first time I met Galen's parents, his mother greeted me with a genuine hug and a tear in her eye. Galen's mother, Debbie Brantley, has never said an ugly word to me. Debbie would be described as a patient, kind, and giving person. Like her son, she can fix just about anything she gets her hands on! Galen's father, Bill Brantley, is a polite, sincere person with a keen memory for his age. Debbie and Bill make great neighbors. If something goes wrong, you can certainly count on them to lend a helping hand.

On Sunday, we went to Galen's church and took a picnic lunch on a hike at Beaver's Bend, a state park in eastern Oklahoma that attracts thousands of tourists ~~each year~~yearly. During the hike, we stopped for lunch, and Galen got down on one knee and asked me to marry him. Though the proposal was a surprise, I had waited so long for that day to finally come! So, of course, I said, "Yes!" As I continually looked at my silver engagement ring with a diamond that sparkled, I realized that marriage was actually going to become a reality for me after all these years of waiting. Galen announced to his family on Christmas day that we would get~~be getting~~ married. The same day, I shared with Galen's family some crucial advice ~~that~~ my mother told her guests at her fiftieth wedding anniversary: "Show your mate the same grace and forgiveness that Christ has shown you." We should ALL keep that in mind. Not ~~too~~ long after Galen proposed, I phoned Anna to tell her the news. I remember saying to her with tears of gratitude, "God keeps His promises." Anna cried with me; we both had prayed for so long for that special man to come into my life.

Planning ~~The~~the Wedding

Shortly after Galen's proposal, we started looking online for wedding dresses. There were so many to choose from, and many were overpriced. It was difficult finding a modest white wedding dress. Some of the dresses online were "open in the back," meaning that too much of a woman's bare back would be showing. Galen told me he would forget his wedding vows if too much of my back was showing, and I certainly didn't want my husband to forget his vows during the wedding ceremony!!

After a few days of visiting Galen and his family, I flew back to TN. The wedding date was set for April 13th, 2019. Fortunately, my sister Penny ~~is a former wedding coordinator and~~, a former wedding coordinator, agreed to decorate for the wedding and reception. Galen's favorite color is purple, so we chose purple and lavender ~~as our colors~~ for the wedding and reception. We chose purple because it represents Christ.

On a more serious note, before we met in person, I explained to Galen that I was still a virgin. Galen also shared with me that he, too, was still a virgin. Truthfully, I did not believe him the first time he told me. I thought, "He's a forty-year-old man," and corresponding with him on the internet, I certainly had my doubts. However, when he came to visit me in TN in November, he told me again, this time in person. When he told me a second time, I knew he was indeed telling the truth. There are a number of Christians who choose abstinence before marriage. So, ladies and gentlemen, there's still hope for single believers ~~p~~who ~~are~~ praying for spouses who have kept themselves pure. *Acts 15:29* says*, "that you abstain from things offered to idols, from blood, from things strangled, and from sexual immorality."* I believe it was a miracle from God that Galen and I found each other.

There were many fine memories I had with the foster children, as well as some "not-so-fine memories." After months of trying to work almost forty hours a week plus foster parenting, my immune system was weakened. I endured sickness after sickness, and Anna was concerned for me as well as the boys. ~~She~~ Finally, she and her husband both concluded ~~came to the conclusion~~ that the boys should be placed in another home. Galen said, "You better not be sick again." After Anna told me that she thought the boys should be placed in another home, I knew something needed to change. Anna had prayed the boys would be reunited with their birth mother. She and I both believed that the birth mother deserved a second chance, and after eight months, the judge ruled that the boys could live with her again!

On Friday, February 8th, 2019, I took the boys to their mother's home along with their belongings. I didn't think it would be difficult to give the boys back, but they boys had become emotionally attached to me. The toddler acted uneasy as I set him down to walk. The next day there were still plenty of baby supplies that needed to be given to the mother. Then on Sunday, Glenda and I took over a basket of items we had put together. After I said goodbye and shut the door, I could hear the infant crying for me. Tears welled up in my eyes as I walked away from their home and got into the vehicle with Glenda. Foster parenting was a good experience that taught me many things, but it was honestly a very demandingdifficult task for a single person.

From February 8th to April 13th, I had a little over two months to prepare for a wedding. My pastor agreed to marry Galen and me; however, he required that we have marriage counseling before the wedding ceremony. Therefore, I would recommend any dating couple who is considering marriage tothat any dating couple considering marriage read *101 Questions to ask Before You Get Engaged* by Norman Wright. 1 The book covers many important topics that should be discussed before you say, "I do." Some questions that Norman mentions include the following:

- If you have children, how will your discipline be the same, and how will it be different than what you experienced?
- To what degree are you a saver or a spender when it comes to money?
- What dreams and aspirations do you have?
- What do you think are God's purposes for marriage?
- What are your beliefs about pornography, and to what degree has this ever been a part of your life? How recently?
- If I were a doctor and you were describing your medical history for me, what would it entail?
- How would you keep your romance alive if you were to marry?
- How do you handle stress and frustration?
- How would you handle holidays, birthdays, special occasions, and so on when it comes to your two families?
- When you marry, do you want children? If so, how many? Are you

open to adoption? What training have you had to be a parent or stepparent?
- Describe how you came to know the Lord. When was it? Who was involved? Where did it take place? How has your life changed?
- What has been your experience with alcohol or drugs in the past and at the present time?
- Politically, where do you find yourself - liberal, middle-of-the-road, conservative, ultra-conservative?
- Do you like animals? What animal would you love to have as a pet that you don't or can't have at this time? How would you work it out if your partner wanted an animal and you didn't?

Depending on the person, some of the questions in the book may be difficult to ask or answer. But to be fair to both parties, it is crucial to know certain information ahead of time.

During our premarital counseling, Robert Russell gave excellent advice: if a couple is not in agreement on an important decision, ~~then~~ they should wait before making a decision.

Galen and I made plans for him to fly to TN for Valentine's Day, but little did we know how the events would unfold before us. It would be the first time ever ~~ever~~ that Galen would wear a black suit, and I was looking forward to having a handsome man pick me up for Valentine's dinner. In eastern OK, the accepted attire for a wedding ceremony, church service, and special occasion include blue jeans, cowboy boots, and plaid shirts, so Galen had to practice tying a tie several times. On February 14th, 2019, I received another peculiar phone call from Galen, informing me that he had missed his flight. I responded by letting him know that I hoped he would not miss his flight for the wedding! We definite~~certain~~ly didn't want missing flights to become a habit for him. Galen had looked at the itinerary for my flight in March instead of double-checking his flight times for February. We prayed over the phone, and I assured him he could fly standby, but the flight took him to North Carolina! He then spent $360 for a rental vehicle to travel from Charlotte, NC, to Bristol, TN, arriving in Bristol early Friday morning.

Galen hasn't had good luck with flying; something usually goes wrong! That evening, I anticipated eating at a fine Italian restaurant. But I would have to celebrate Valentine's Day a day late, which I didn't mind too much. However, once we arrived at the Italian restaurant, a lady met us near the entrance to inform us that we would not be able to eat there due to technical problems. Really??? I guessed things couldn't get much worse, so we settled for Olive Garden. Shortly after our meal, Galen met my parents for the first time. Mother blurted out with excitement, "You're going to give us lots of grandbabies." She sure had a way of speaking her mind!

In March 2019, I again flew to OK to visit Galen. We met Galen's good friend Weylin and his wife for supper one evening. Galen and Weylin have known each other since high school. Weylin was the type of person that would do just about anything you asked of him, and he was a reliable, trustworthy individual. He introduced me to his wife, Shelby, a kind, hospitable woman. Galen chose Weylin to be his best man for the wedding ceremony.

Due to his experiences with previous flights, Galen was going to make sure he did not miss the flight to his own wedding! He-So, he flew into the Tri-Cities airport on the Thursday before the ceremony and plannedmade plans to rent a pick-up truck for the honeymoon. Though he had a high limit on his debit card, the rental company would not allow Galen to use it to pay for the truck rental. So, Galen rode home with me to ask my dad if he could borrow his credit card for the truck rental! Dad gladly entrusted Galen with his credit card; Galen assured Dad he would pay him back. Now Galen was almost completely ready for the honeymoon!

My sister Doreen was chosen to be the maid of honor. There were a number of people who helped decorate for the wedding. Many friends and relatives came to the wedding. Beforehand, Anna and I prayed that God would be glorified through the ceremony, and He most certainly was. We hoped that people would see how forgiving and gracious God is. Silly things happen, even on wedding days: after the reception, I forgot to take my suitcase with me when Galen and I left for our honeymoon! A witty elderly woman said, "You don't need clothes for the honeymoon!"

Life in Oklahoma

Moving away from my family and a good-sized city was not always easy; adjusting to life in the rural part of OK had ~~its~~ occasional difficulties. I quickly learned that males and females often think differently, but there are many pleasant things to enjoy near my new home. Galen's hobbies include hunting, rifle making, and long-range shooting. In regards to hunting, God gave us dominion over the fish of the sea and the birds of the air. I am not opposed to hunting animals for food; however, I will say that I am not a fan of killing an animal for sport, for the Bible teaches us not to waste. On November 30th, 2019, Galen and I went hunting the day after Thanksgiving. After sitting still for a long time, I started to dose off while Galen kept a watchful eye. Shortly before dusk, two female deer came to graze just yards away from where we were sitting quietly. Galen motioned towards me, so I slowly aimed my rifle and fired, missing the first shot. Luckily, the doe was still standing there, so I aimed a second time and fired. This time the bullet hit her. Before ~~I went~~ hunting, I prayed that God would provide deer for us; shortly afterward, He answered my prayer. Living with a hunter, I have eaten different types of wildlife meat - deer, elk, squirrel, and beaver. Since I've been married, I have killed three deer. It is a practical way to bring food to the table.

Many people believe the United States of America is the greatest nation in the world. It certainly has gorgeous scenery, and I understand why men ~~have~~ sacrificed their lives for this country. In June 2020, my husband and I took a vacation trip to Colorado. I remember my pastor saying, "Creation screams that there is a God." We can certainly see evidence of a magnificent Creator in the majestic mountains, deep blue lakes, quiet gurgling creeks, desert sunsets, inquisitive animals, and the complexity of the human body. In Colorado, we were lucky enough to see mountain goats, moose, deer, foxes, bears, and hummingbirds. One day while we were ~~den we were~~ driving on a back road, I saw a black bear standing on its hind legs. At first, I thought it was a statue, but then the bear started to run for safety! Two cubs followed after the bear, so we knew it was a female bear. I wish I had taken a picture of the bears!

My Favorite Wildlife Picture Taken ~~In~~in Colorado

Fawns Grazing ~~In~~in Our Yard

Galen and I in Colorado

Answered Prayer

Followers of Christ know the importance of prayer. So, I would like to share an amazing story of how quickly the Lord answered Anna's prayer. On one particular day in September 2020, Anna prayed, "Lord, please let Sarai meet her husband today." Sarai, Anna's youngest daughter, went on a date that very day and met a quite fine young Christian man. Almost one year later, that same young man married Sarai! They had a beautiful wedding ceremony just minutes from Sarai's home. During the wedding ceremony, Sarai mentioned that they could serve God better by being married. Sometimes our prayers are answered that very day, but at other times, it's weeks, months, or even years later.

Unexpected Trials

Life brings unexpected challenges. Job in the Bible probably didn't expect his sons, daughters, and animals would be killed. When I was thirty-eight, we found out that my brother's wife, Lori had cancer. She was a pretty, joyful, humorous woman who tended to look on the bright side of things. Lori had home-schooled her children and done a fine job raising them. She taught her children good manners, kindness, responsibility, and many other important things. On March 26th, 2021, my mother, my three sisters (Anna, Penny, Doreen), Lori, and I met at Anna's house to pray. Anna, who's considered a spiritual mentor, begged God to heal Lori from her cancer. We wept for Lori and asked God for a miracle. Those of us who have lived long enough know that His answer is sometimes "no." And yet, He IS still just. I remember receiving a text from Lori on July 13th, 2021, hinting to my sisters and me that she didn't have very long to live, but she hoped to at least make it to her daughter's wedding. Lori had been a part of our family for over thirty years, and it was difficult to accept the fact that she would not live much longer. Scripture was an essential part of her life; on several occasions, she sent my sisters and me encouraging verses through text messages. In fact, it was Lori who came up with the idea of expressing thankfulness in weekly texts.

On Friday, July 30th, 2021, people gathered at Lori's house to pray for her. By this point, her organs had started to shut down though she was still breathing. Her hair was now gray, and her skin had turned orange. At the gathering, my brother Robert explained that when Lori's doctors gave her discouraging information about cancer, she would look at the doctors, smile, and say, "My life belongs to Jesus Christ." Hours before her death, I was able to spend some time alone with her. We knew she loved Scripture, so I read some verses to her, not knowing that would be the last time I spoke to her in person. She died that evening, on August 2nd, 2021. Lori had suffered long enough and was ready to meet her Savior. Despite the heartache of losing his wife, Robert remained calm and met with people to prepare for the funeral.

Four months after Lori's death, Galen and I took a trip to visit Robert and his two sons, Kyle and Weston. They were all happy to see us and eager to talk. I saw no anger or bitterness in Robert, Kyle or Weston, despite ~~the fact that~~ Lori <u>being gone.</u>~~was gone.~~ God's goodness is shown in their lives. The words of the song "Evidence" by Josh Baldwin come to my mind: the evidence of God's goodness is in my life and is evident in the lives of others.

I could spend lots of time talking about my amazing husband: Galen is kind, considerate, witty, wise, and solid in his faith. He is God's precious gift to me. The Lord <u>graciously game</u> ~~was very gracious to give~~ me a husband like Galen, for I certainly don't deserve him. That is why I titled my book, *Undeserving Grace*.

• Wright, Norman. *101 Questions to ask Before You Get Engaged.* (Harvest House Publishers, 2

About ~~The~~the Author

Chanel Brantley resides with her husband, Galen Brantley, in Oklahoma. She has served at Christian camps in Tennessee and North Carolina during the summer for several years. Chanel has taught at children's Bible clubs in Pennsylvania and Oklahoma. She enjoys camping, hunting, swimming, and hiking for recreation.

Made in the USA
Middletown, DE
20 December 2022

19896222R00020